GRAPHIC L

Lexi

Carol Holliday & Jo Browning Wroe

Illustrated by Tim Evans

First published in 2016 by

Speechmark Publishing Ltd

2nd Floor, 5 Thomas More Square, London E1W 1YW, UK

Tel: +44 (0)845 034 4610 Fax: +44 (0)845 034 4649

www.speechmark.net

Designed and typeset by Moo Creative (Luton)

002-6014/Printed in the United Kingdom by CMP (uk) Ltd

British Library Cataloguing in Publication Data

A catalogue record for this book is available from the British Library

ISBN 978 1 90930 166 5

Woodland
CARBON
www.woodlandcarbon.co.uk
16CMPUKL
Printed on Carbon Captured paper

1

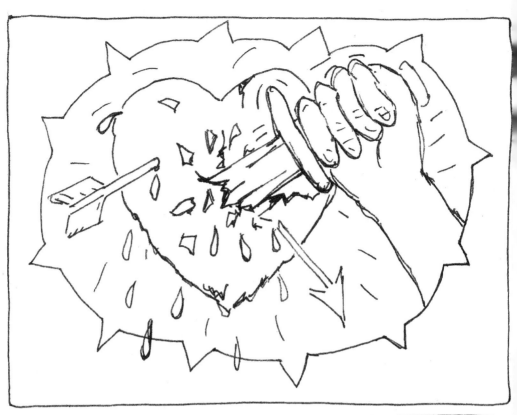

9

18

19

WHAT WAS IT LIKE FOR YOU WORKING WITH THAT PAINTING?

IT WAS TOUGH BUT I'M GLAD I DID IT. I'M REALLY TIRED.

YOU'VE WORKED REALLY HARD TODAY. EMOTIONAL WORK IS TIRING

BEING IN THE SAME CLASS AS JAKE AND CHLOE IS GOING TO BE REALLY PAINFUL.

AND IT'S GOING TO BRING UP OTHER PAINFUL FEELINGS FROM THE PAST...

..BUT WE CAN WORK WITH THOSE FEELINGS AND THINK ABOUT THEM HERE.

23

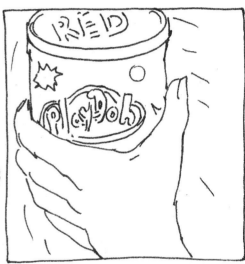

24

29

31

43

44

LATER

I'M HAPPY FOR YOU MUM BUT I'M AFRAID I'LL LOSE YOU AND FEEL LEFT OUT. I SOMETIMES FEEL LIKE THAT AT DAD'S

OF COURSE! WHY DIDN'T I SEE IT?

IF YOU FEEL LIKE THAT, PROMISE TO TELL ME?

I WILL.

49